Table of Contents

Table of Contents

WINE *for* BUSINESSPEOPLE
—— 100 ——

THE CASE
for WINE

William J. Libby

ISBN-13: 978-1470085544

Copyright © 2012 by William J. Libby

Published in the United States by Libby Communications
Muskegon, Michigan.

The *Wine for Businesspeople 100* series is a trademark of
Libby Communications.

Testimonials

Read what businesspeople are saying about *Wine for Businesspeople 100: The Case for Wine*

"*The Case for Wine* steered me to a higher level of respect for the ability of wine to create an atmosphere where you can really connect with people."

> Mark McNeely
> Marketing Manager
> TOSHIBA
> West Allis, WI

"U.S. wine consumption has grown steadily for the last two decades. This trend is driven by the affluent, highly educated and well-travelled—a good description of businesspeople. Bill Libby's book is timely."

> Howard Gordon
> Principal
> GRFI Ltd. Market Insight Practice
> Chicago, IL

"Doing business internationally virtually guarantees you will be working with a lot of people who enjoy wine at business meals. In these kinds of circumstances, knowing your way around a wine list is invaluable."

> John Jenkins
> Director, Business Excellence
> RTI International Metals, Inc.
> Houston, TX

"Bill Libby spotlights the role entertaining with wine plays in creating and maintaining a long-term bond between businesspeople and customers. His wine-blooper stories underscore the importance of doing wine right."

John W. Manchester
Partner
The Manchester Co., Inc.
Hartland, MI

"Many business leaders recognize that confidence when handling wine sends a signal of sophistication, social accomplishment and savoir-faire. For this reason, *The Case for Wine* is a book I will use as an advertisement for my wine-education firm, Wine Wise Consulting."

Megan Wiig
Principal
Wine Wise Consulting
New York, NY

"Bill Libby's case histories about wine offer some telling examples of senior businesspeople who muffed their attempts to bring wine into a business gathering. I know from personal experience that the outcomes of senior managers' behavior can ding employees' morale, as well as their attitude toward the company that employs them."

Peter Krupp
Owner
Peter Krupp Photography
Corvallis, OR

"When I entertain I like to go to BYOB restaurants. They tend to have interesting food and I can practice pairing wines with out-of-the-ordinary ethnic dishes. Most businesspeople don't do this, so it's a way for me to stand out and be memorable compared to people who entertain in more traditional ways."

Raymond A. Osborne
Free-lance Writer
Chicago, IL

"You never know when a business-entertainment opportunity will arise where knowing about wine would be helpful. Bill Libby's *The Case for Wine* points the way to success with a lot of easy-to-use tips for learning about wine."

Charles Orman
Product Support Representative
Daily Equipment Company
Pearl, MS

"At senior leadership levels, wine is often a key part of entertaining. For this reason, it is particularly valuable for a business leader to know as much about wine as her most wine-savvy associates or guests."

Sarah J. Clark
Director
HR Technology, North America
Towers Watson
Chicago, IL

"As a salesman, I need to be able to get on the wavelength of every customer and prospect. When I'm selling someone who likes wine, knowing about wine is a huge plus."

Joseph Dammann
Sales Engineer
Fabcon
Savage, MN

"Once, at a business dinner, a former boss was talking to our customer and just handed the wine list to me, saying 'Pick a nice wine for us.' I had no idea what to do then. Now I do."

Steve Sullivan
Artist/Entrepreneur
Los Angeles, CA

To read reviews of *Wine for Businesspeople 100: The Case for Wine*,
log onto: www.amazon.com

Dedication

I dedicate this book to Marcia, my wife, who has taught me more about wine than anyone. I also dedicate it to my many wine mentors, clients and associates who have taught me the rest of what I know about wine and how to use it to entertain effectively in business. You know who you are. Your friendship, goodwill and support have made my career a joy and I feel lucky to have had the opportunity to work with you and, frequently, to share wine with you as well.

CHAPTER I

The Wonderful World of Wine Bloopers

I hold these truths to be demonstrable:

> *Businesspeople want to be successful.*
> *Wine knowledge can help businesspeople be successful.*
> *Therefore, businesspeople can benefit from acquiring wine knowledge.*

That's my thesis in a nutshell.

The opposite of wine knowledge is wine ignorance. There is plenty of wine ignorance to go around. I know. I once had more than my fair share.

Simply stated, wine ignorance—and ignorance of the nuances of dining etiquette—can make you look dumb. Real dumb. They made me feel dumb once and, in a very direct way, business was to blame. First, the backstory.

Not long after I was hired at a big advertising agency I was invited to a restaurant on Chicago's Gold Coast.

My host, an advertising salesman, recommended I try his favorite fish dish and a wine he vouched would go well with it. When the meal was served, a bandaged object at the edge of each plate caught my attention.

Not wanting to display my ignorance I stalled, fiddling with my napkin, watching my host to see what he did with it. The object was hemispheric, wrapped in an opaque gauze, with a small fastener crimping the material together tightly at the top. I'd never seen anything like it in my life and I was wary.

Out of the corner of my eye, I watched my host pick up the object, position it over his fish and squeeze. With practiced movements he distributed lemon juice evenly over his fish. The fragrance of the lemon answered the question "What?"

Not wanting to look like this was the first time I was ever in a really fancy restaurant (which in truth it was) I copied his action. I gave the lemon a good squeeze and, when it had yielded its juice, I turned it over for inspection. Trapped in the gauze were three lemon seeds. Now I knew the "Why?"

A rheostat turned up in my mind illuminating the experience, an orchestra swelled, and I witnessed an image of myself ascending to a higher rung on the ladder of life. Ah, nice feeling.

The restaurant impressed me so much that I determined to take my soon-to-be wife there on our planned, in-town honeymoon only a few weeks away. I wanted to repeat the experience with her. I could hardly wait.

The repeat visit was marred by a wine blooper. After studying the wine list, and feeling in an expansive mood, my eye was hooked by one of the Champagne options. Not one of those regular wimpy bottles, but a magnum, a real live magnum of French Champagne, right there on the list. I had a vague impression that a magnum was bigger than a regular bottle, but had no idea exactly how much bigger. However, on the night after my wedding night, I wanted big.

"We'll have the magnum of Champagne," I said decisively.

The waiter raised one eyebrow, nodded, got the magnum and presented it to me. People at other tables glanced over to observe the ceremony. A magnum, I discovered, is twice the size of a normal bottle.

My brand-new wife and the waiter both looked at me expectantly.

My heart sank. I had stepped out with a most wonderful expectation and all at once there was nothing under my feet. I had screwed up. The magnum contained way more Champagne than two people should drink. I felt myself falling, if not literally, at least figuratively, in the eyes of two people—one of them a pretty significant person at an important moment in our lives.

Wine Fact

The United States of America is projected to become the world's largest consumer of wine in 2012. The latest official information on the wine race is from www.wineinstitute.org

Wine Consumption by Volume, 2009[1]
(Liters 000)

France:.............2,913,800
U.S.:.................2,752,140
Italy: 2,450,000

"I think that may be a little more Champagne than we need," my wife said.

"Would the standard bottle suit you," the waiter asked deferentially? He included my wife in the question, not only me. She knew what she was doing. I didn't.

She nodded. He departed.

I remember looking around the restaurant. The setting was everything it could possibly be—the chairs plush and comfortable, the lighting just so, the linen crisp, the silver bright, the crystal dazzling. The food was superb and the waiters professional to a fault. It was exactly the kind of restaurant I wanted to do business in regularly for the rest of my career. At that moment it was borne home to me that I had much to learn before I could walk this terroir confidently.

Years later the memory of this blooper can return and make me wince. Especially when I imagine the waiter gleefully recounting the incident to his colleagues at the close of business.

INSIGHT

There is a big difference between being a guest and being a host.

You don't have to know much if you are someone's valued guest. A practiced host will guide the way and a novice can learn much by merely paying attention.

However, a little knowledge is a dangerous thing. The experience of being a guest does not transform one into an accomplished host. Like others I know who have embarrassed themselves with a wine blooper, I vowed to learn about wine.

CHAPTER II

Wine Bloopers: Junior & Senior Moments

This book has three goals: First, to make the case that wine knowledge helps people succeed in business. Second, to document how poor wine skills can damage the way an individual—and sometimes even a company—is perceived. And third, to inspire in you a desire to learn about wine. Acquiring even a limited understanding of wine basics can give you the confidence to make business entertainment a truly effective business tool. Note well: if your career is progressing nicely, sooner or later you and wine will cross paths.

Consider these hip-pocket case histories.

1. A woman of a certain age who purchases enormous amounts of printing at last agrees to meet Drew, a young man who sells printing services. After considerable persistence, he finally succeeds in persuading her to have lunch with him.

   Drew has heard on the grapevine that she enjoys a glass or two of wine at lunch, so, thoughtful prospective supplier that he is, he asks her, after they are seated in the restaurant, if she would like some wine.

   "Yes," she says.

   Upon being handed the wine list and studying it uncomprehendingly for a while, he asks: "What kind of wine would you like?"

   "Impress me," she says.

2. George, an inventor, drives one dark and stormy evening to a gathering of "angels," where people with ideas can meet people with money.

   He has researched local investors likely to be at the event, and, while working the room during the cocktail hour before the presentations, he spots not one, but two of these angels in a corner talking together.

George raises the glass of beer he bought at the cash bar and takes a sip. He notices that the two men he most wants to speak to are holding long-stemmed glasses containing a dark-red liquid. He further notices that most of the other people in the room are, like himself, drinking beer or what may or may not be a mixed drink.

The inventor returns to the bar area, placing his far-from-finished beer on a tray for empties. He gets back in line to order a glass of wine. While waiting, he turns a few thoughts over in his mind. One thought is that when he walks up to the two wine drinkers, he wants to make an immediate impression that he is their kind of guy. Another thought is that he is taking a risk. He is a beer drinker; he knows nothing about wine.

When it is his turn, he asks the bartender about his wine options.

"Red or white."

George orders red and asks: "What can you tell me about this wine?"

Looking surprised at the question, the bartender finishes pouring the wine, then scans the label. "It's a Cabernet Sauvignon from Napa," he says, as if that settles the matter.

"Do you know anything else about it?"

The bartender shakes his head and turns his gaze to the next customer. The inventor circumnavigates the room in the direction of the two angels, eventually getting close enough to hear their conversation.

Both men stop talking and stare at the young man who has encroached on their space. Surprised by their abrupt silence and suddenly guarded gazes, the young man is momentarily at a loss for words. One angel looks at the wine glass in his hand and drawls: "So…what do you think of the Cab?"

3. A young salesman named Arthur is hosting a dinner at a famous steakhouse near the headquarters of an important customer. Three people from his company and five from the customer's firm have gathered in a private dining room to celebrate the successful completion of a project.

The salesman's boss and the top person on the customer's team are outdoing themselves complimenting each other's company when my friend interrupts to ask his guest, who has a reputation as a wine maven: "Would you like to pick the wine?"

The customer waves off the opportunity by pointing at the wine list in Arthur's hand and saying genially: "No, no! You're the host!" He returns to his conversation with the young man's boss.

Arthur knows a little something about wine. One person on whom he calls is fond of White Zinfandel and always orders it when they go to that customer's favorite restaurant. In addition, he has recently been to dinner at an associate's house where he was served a Riesling. His host had been very keen on the Riesling and the name of the wine stuck in his mind.

Building on what he knows, Arthur orders a bottle of each to drink with the hors d'oeuvres. When the servers approach the group to hand out glasses and pour wine for the guests, the wine bearer holds the two bottles up before the highest-ranking customer. "Which would you like, sir?"

The customer looks at the options, frowns, thinks for a moment, then whispers tactfully to the server: "Actually, I'd like to see the wine list."

*   *   *

Like me decades ago, most young people entering the business world have little or no knowledge about wine. This may pose a problem for them during encounters with senior executives who know wine and prefer it to other beverages. But junior executives are not the only ones who are wine-challenged. Next, let's consider a series of wine stories involving senior executives.

*   *   *

4. An engineer is hired by a high-tech manufacturing company. As a signal of the critical role he is expected to play at the company, the young man and his wife are invited to dinner at a highly regarded restaurant by Frederick, one of the company's vice presidents. The dinner is the capstone event in bringing the new hire on board.

Fresh out of college, with roots in small-town America, the new man and his wife are unfamiliar with wine. They watch as the VP examines the bottle he has ordered and, after tasting it, nods his approval to the server.

When his guests are served, the host raises a toast.

"Welcome aboard!" says Frederick.

The young couple clink glasses with their host and take a sip.

As the wine hits their taste buds, the youngsters exchange surreptitious glances. Even though they have no experience with wine, it is not hard for them to know that the wine tastes bad. Their taste buds tell them instantly that the brackish liquid in their mouths is not pleasant to drink.

Smiling awkwardly, they look at their host. Frederick smiles back. The couple wait, innocently entertaining the expectation that the host will call the waiter over to do something about the wine. But he does not. The evening proceeds. Frederick drinks his share of the wine dutifully and the young couple make a show of taking polite-pretend sips at long intervals and soldier through the meal with multiple refills of their water glasses. The bottle is still half full—and the guests' wine glasses almost full—when the meal ends. The host appears not to notice the rejected wine.

5. Hilda, an HR manager, takes her staff of three and their spouses to dinner in recognition of their efforts over a year punctuated by many accomplishments. As the group assembles in the foyer of a private dining room, the boss orders a nice bottle of wine to go with the hors d'oeuvres being carried around on trays. The evening is off to a great start.

With eight people to serve, the bottle is deftly poured out to accommodate all the drinkers. After a discrete interval (this is, after all, a good restaurant) the server asks the host if she would like him to serve another bottle.

"Oh, no," answers the host, as if that were the strangest thing she could imagine. "That's all the wine we'll be having this evening!"

6. Dick, the founder, owner, CEO and cutting edge of a large real estate firm, sponsors a celebratory dinner

Wine Fact

The U.S. is the world's fourth largest wine producer.

Wine Production by Volume, 2009[2]
(Liters 000)

France:	4,700,000
Italy:	4,600,000
Spain:	3,800,000
U.S.:	2,777,200

for two management teams, one from his firm and another from a company he has just acquired. The two teams are brought together for a get-acquainted event. The idea is to waste no time in getting down to the task of team building, as the two groups will soon be working together. The CEO of the acquiring company has completed a good deal and is in the mood to party. Unlike the manager in my previous example, he is not about to let his guests suffer a no-wine-with-dinner experience. He personally controls the wine ordering, and does it with the largess of someone who both approves his own expense account and is eager to communicate his company's work-hard/play-hard/live-well philosophy.

Unfortunately for his guests, a number of whom know a bit about wine, their host picks wines by hop-scotching randomly around a 12-page wine list the way a first-time visitor to a race track might impulsively select horses from the *Daily Racing Form*. This self-made man created his own success by trusting his instincts. True to character, he sought no one's counsel regarding his wine selections as he repeatedly called out for "More wine!"

As wine after expensive wine arrives—wines poorly matched with the foods being served—covert and knowing glances begin to be shared around the table. The wine-savvy on both teams comment among themselves about "pairings from hell." This topic provides much of the conversational content among those out of earshot of the boss. The CEO, known to combine a dislike of personal criticism with a habit of confident assertiveness when dealing with people of opposing viewpoints, attracted no comments that might have improved his wine selections.

INSIGHT

Bill's First Law of Wine in Business is that, sooner or later, wine will spill into the business lives of junior and senior people—and someone will be watching to observe how they handle themselves.

Bill's Corollary to the First Law of Wine in Business is that ignorance of this law is no excuse.

CHAPTER III

How Wine Puts You in the Spotlight

Whatever you know about wine, and whatever your attitude toward your fund of knowledge, these six stories show that wine can suddenly offer an opportunity to look good—or not so good.

Let's revisit these stories to see how they turned out and discover what they have to tell us about wine in business.

"Impress me!"

In my first story, Drew had no idea what might be involved in impressing his luncheon companion. He knew little about wine beyond knowing that Chardonnay existed and that it was a white wine. He knew this because his girlfriend liked Chardonnay and drank a glass of it occasionally when they dined out together.

Drew resumed his study of the wine list, but remained at a loss as to how to impress his guest. As the interval of indecision began to stretch out uncomfortably, Drew impulsively ordered the most expensive bottle of Chardonnay on the menu. For his lunch that day, he ordered a cheeseburger, his favorite restaurant meal.

The lunch went pleasantly enough. He remembered his guest talked about wine only briefly before steering the conversation to other topics. Drew realized, while reflecting later that day, that these were probably topics on which his prospective customer decided he might have something to contribute. When he tried to talk business, his companion always turned the conversation back to non-business subjects. There was another warning sign. At the end of lunch, Drew was knocked off balance when his guest insisted on paying.

Drew had a bad feeling about being transformed from a host into a guest. That bad feeling was later amplified when his prospect avoided his string of follow-up phone calls. Eventually, he crossed the woman and her company off his list of viable prospects and moved on.

What did the woman really think of Drew and his ability to supply her printing needs? Drew never found out. He did, however, suspect that his lack of wine skill played a role in his failure to earn an opportunity to work with the woman's company.

In a later conversation with one of the senior salesmen at his company, Drew complained about the way his prospect's eccentric behavior prevented him from getting a fair hearing. At the end of his complaint, the senior salesman invited Drew to look at the situation from his prospect's point of view.

"A prospective customer is under no obligation to adapt herself to us," he said. "You were asking for an opportunity to enter her world. You knew beforehand she liked wine, but were not really prepared to deal with this part of her world. All suppliers get qualified in one way or another. One of her ways may be to see if the person she'll have to deal with enjoys wine. You had neither the listening skills to pick up her signals to chitchat on a subject of interest to her, nor the experience to engage her in a wine conversation. Maybe she just decided to keep looking for someone else who could connect with her better."

Based on this conversation, Drew started to teach himself about wine and to practice using what he learned.

INSIGHT

People like doing business with others who share their interests.

Some, maybe many, of the people with the authority to buy your product or service, support your cause, or influence the direction of legislation that affects your company or your client's organization, have made wine a part of their lives. All other things being equal, they may simply prefer to deal with people who share this interest.

Buy a bottle of wine to go with an upcoming dinner at home. Your local wine seller can help you pick a wine for a specific dish until you get the hang of pairing wine with food. Pay attention to it while drinking it. In your opinion, do the food and the wine enhance each other? Your answer to this question can lay the cornerstone of a potent new skill for business entertaining.

"What do you think of the Cab?"

Let's resume where we left off with George, the inventor. When asked by one of the angel investors what he thought of the "Cab," he was taken aback, although he is sure his poker-playing skills insured that he did not show it. He picked right up on the meaning of "Cab," although he had never heard the word used to refer to anything other than a vehicle for hire. He raised the glass a little above eye height and scrutinized its contents against the light for a moment, a feint that gave him a few precious seconds to rummage around in his brain for something to say.

"Any Cab in a storm," he blurted.

George tells me he has no idea how this rejoinder simultaneously popped into his head and out of his mouth, but it got him out of the spot he was in. The other angel chirped, "Any Port, too!" They all had a hearty laugh at this witticism and, after a pro forma exchange about the dreadful weather, George skillfully set up an opportunity to shift the conversation to his invention, which, oddly enough, involved reducing the amount of beer wasted when served from kegs.

Later, when assessing his performance in light of the evening's outcome, which produced nothing more than faint praise for his invention among people with money to invest, George turned the "Cab" incident over again and again in his mind. The connection between desirable business contacts and wine drinking suggested to him that this might not be the last time he would run into wine drinkers in the course of trying to sell his innovation. He wondered if the evening might have gone differently had he been able to hold his own in a serious conversation about wine. If he could talk about wine with some authority, he thought, the subject of wine might have become a bridge to a conversation about beer. If he could have related his idea to the angel investor within the framework of the angel's interests rather than his interests, perhaps the conversation would have taken a turn in a different direction.

However, lacking experience with wine, George did not have the raw material to build that bridge. Tantalizing as the potential connection between wine and beer was, George did not have the background to make an inspired connection linking the investor's interest in wine to his innovation in dispensing beer.

Like Drew, once the downside of not knowing much about wine became apparent to him, George reconsidered why he always avoided having anything to do with wine. He concluded that his rivalry with his brother, who was a wine drinker, lay at the root of his stance. It was one of the ways he differentiated himself from his brother.

The next time he met his brother, George mentioned his experience at the angels' event and, after talking only a short while, found his brother a source of valuable information about wine in general and its place in business in particular. Ever since, George has been learning about wine from his brother and—to his surprise—enjoying the experience.

INSIGHT

The wine-savvy may use wine as one of their ways to find out what kind of person you are.

As a rule of thumb, it is safe to assume that people with capital to invest or budgets to expend could also be people with a taste for wine. There is a correlation between affluence and wine. As The Economist *reported, "Richer people see wine as more upmarket..."[3]*

Keep track of the wines you drink. Your restaurant receipt may provide useful information such as date consumed, price and, perhaps, at better restaurants, even the name and vintage of the wine. You can use your cell phone, if it is so equipped, to snap a picture of the label. This task takes no more than a few seconds and has the added benefit of sharpening your photographic skills at the same time it helps build your personal reference material about wine. Paying attention to wine signals your interest in the finer things in life. There are also mobile phone apps that enable you to build a personal body of wine information.

"Actually, I'd like to see the wine list."

You might consider the two previous stories as "before-the-sale" examples. The third example of a young person with a wine deficit involves a situation based on an existing and quite solid business relationship.

In this instance, Arthur, the young sales engineer, knew a bit about wine. Specifically, he had experienced two wines and used what he knew to respond to the challenge of selecting wines for the group. When he watched the customer reject his picks, he knew he had not done a satisfactory job in the eyes of an important person. He knew he had missed something. Arthur is not the kind of person to miss much in business. However, prior to this experience, he simply never viewed competence with wine as part of his job description. This instance impressed upon him that, indirectly, it was very much a part of his job description.

When the third wine arrived, the customer called Arthur over, saying: "We are in the best steak joint in the whole state. Everybody will probably order steak tonight because this restaurant is famous for it." He called for a clean glass for the young man.

"Try this wine. Later, when you are eating the signature steak I suspect you will order, check out how nicely this wine goes with what's on your plate. If you pay attention to what you are eating and drinking, I think you'll agree that the wine I picked is a better wine in general and also a better match up for the steaks most of us will eat later."

Arthur followed this advice and found himself in agreement. That hard-nosed, upper-echelon, highly demanding businesspeople might pay passionate attention to pairing food and wine was a new concept for Arthur. He had not encountered an instance of that before.

On the spot, Arthur made a decision to learn about wine. Subsequently, as he pursued this new interest, he discovered that he had many opportunities for wine conversations with his customer, which added a new dimension to their get-togethers. These wine conversations became a permanent thread that ran through the relationship between the two executives over the years. By combining his growing interest in wine with the skills that had already made him good at his job, Arthur found many ways, he tells me, to add a strong personal component to his connection with his customer and, through that more personal relationship, to become more effective at his job.

One lesson in these three examples is that senior business people often know wine, enjoy it frequently, and, when interacting with associates, like to bring wine into the flow of business in appropriate circumstances. This

Wine Fact

74 percent of the wine consumed in the U.S. is produced domestically. 26 percent is imported.[4]

preference for wine provides one good reason for people new to wine to develop a practical skill. It opens the door to conversations with senior people about a topic not confined to, although very useful in, business.

The next three stories focus on the other end of the career timeline: Senior executives who don't do wine well. As these examples show, an interminable evening, with a persistent cloud of awkwardness hovering above it, is guaranteed to materialize when guests feel they must wash down their food with bad wine, the wrong wine, or no wine at all.

INSIGHT

When you work with people who care about wine, it doesn't hurt for you to care about wine, too.

You can strengthen an already healthy relationship by sharing wine. This is especially true when your customer or client likes wines, but it is equally true when your familiarity with wine allows you to play the role of wine guide for someone who knows less than you.

Be on the lookout for opportunities to learn about wine. The Internet is a cornucopia of information. More than 60 percent of the wineries in America have a website. Leading business publications like *The Wall Street Journal* and national newspapers like *The New York Times* routinely have delightfully informative articles on wine. From time to time, so may your local newspaper. Keep your eye peeled for wine news and make a habit of putting to use the information you discover.

"Welcome aboard!"

Frederick, the vice president, apparently did not have the ability to notice that the wine he ordered had gone bad. His guest, newly hired out of college and with no background in wine, would not have felt comfortable challenging the judgment of an executive as old as his grandfather. At the time this incident took place, for all he and his wife knew, this might be the way that particular wine was supposed to taste. One need only think of the Tom Hanks' character in the movie *Big* having his first encounter with caviar.

This is a perfect time to emphasize a crucial point: Introducing wine into an event serves to make that event special. Ordering, approving and consuming wine signals something more than ordinary is going on. At the Wedding in Cana (John 2:1-10) scripture speaks of Jesus turning water into wine, not a pitcher of Margaritas. Wine has a long history as an indicator that something special is transpiring. So when something goes wrong due to the way wine is integrated into an event, the negative fallout is super-sized because of the gaping hole that opens up between expectations and experience.

What makes Frederick's story poignant is that he set out with the best of intentions. He knew the ingredients for making people feel valued. The young engineer's wife was included in the dinner invitation, so she could share along with her husband his feeling of success at landing a good job. The event took place at the area's finest restaurant, so the "welcome aboard" gesture was designed to make a first-rate impression. Lastly, wine was included, so its presence would mark the occasion as a real celebration.

Frederick knew all of these things. He understood their significance. The two things he apparently did not know, as indicated by his behavior, were how to recognize bad wine and what to do about it when he did. Unfortunately, when wine is improperly sealed, air can get into the bottle, oxidizing the wine. And occasionally, bacteria get into the bottle before it is sealed. As a result, the wine becomes "corked." Whatever the cause, the wine Frederick ordered was bad. However, he did nothing about the problem and the evening turned into a poor experience for his guests.

Right up there with the fear of public speaking, is fear of wine. Barbara Insel, citing a Stonebridge Research demographic study, reports "…the way we market wine makes many men feel insecure…Many men feel they never know enough about wine or have enough confidence in their decisions to choose wine in a so-cial situation. The fear of losing face, of being embarrassed by making the 'wrong' choice, is huge."[5]

Was Frederick afraid? Did he fear that he would look like a fool if he tried to reject a wine that might not be bad? Did his fear arise from uncertainty? Did uncertainty make him hesitate? Did hesitation stop him from calling attention to the problem until it was too late?

I don't know. Neither do Frederick's guests. What we do know is that the young engineer wanted to make sure he never put anyone else through the same kind of "celebration." This experience led to his life-long effort to educate himself about wine.

INSIGHT

Wine lapses can inadvertently transform what should be a memorable experi-ence into an unforgettable ordeal.

If subordinates suffer because you don't know enough about wine to spare them a bad time, it's time to master the basics. When you are a host, it is un-seemly to fail in your responsibilities for insuring an evening memorable for the right reasons. If you know nothing about wine, I would suggest that you find a way to work around that shortcoming. You have responsibilities as host and your guests count on you to live up to them.

Get to know your local wine store (the one with employees who can actually sustain an intelligent conversation with you about wine). Every visit can be instructive. Professional wine sellers typically have a range of experience they are happy to share. Serious wine merchants frequently sponsor wine tastings to introduce customers to wines they may never have tried—another way to expand your knowledge.

"That's all the wine we'll be having this evening."

My fifth story has morphed into an enigma of Bermuda-Triangle dimensions for the people involved: It is a mystery no one has ever satisfactorily explained. In one sense, it is not about wine per se; rather it has to do with wine etiquette or maybe just common sense about entertaining. In this story Hilda, the HR department head, clearly wanted to do something special for her team. But for some reason she acted like a strict Federal Reserve Chairman, yanking away the wine bucket just as the party got going. People who thought they were on their way to feeling special suddenly were made to feel emphatically unspecial.

Like the young couple in my previous example, the guests were socially check-mated by the boss's behavior. They were unsure what they could or should do about it. In the circumstances described, all of Hilda's associates would have been willing to pay for their own bottle of wine to accompany dinner. However, to suggest there was a need for that action on the part of guests would have been an implied criticism of Hilda's competence as a host. No one was comfortable taking that step with an aloof and sometimes unpredictable boss.

The person who related Hilda's story to me is someone highly aware of how wine lapses can lead to client-management problems. When she heard about the story, she made a point of discretely investigating the incident with each of Hilda's team members. All confirmed the story and the feeling of having been put in an awkward position.

One said he wondered if Hilda was worried that drinking more than one glass of wine would make it dangerous for her associates to drive home after dinner. "But that's not really a valid concern," he concluded. "We're all married with children, mortgages and current or future college-tuition obligations. We're not the kind of people who have drinking and driving problems."

Another said she thought the decision probably reflected Hilda's business-like approach to everything. "Our mistake was thinking this was a social get-together because our spouses were involved. Hilda probably had a budget for this out-of-the-ordinary event and more wine would have busted the budget."

A third person expanded on the second person's comments, saying, "We all worked hard to make the department look good last year. When she decided to thank us for all our extra effort, she found her gratitude had limits. I think she got ahead of herself with the pricey restaurant she picked, and then decided against using her own money when funds for thanking us all of a sudden got tight."

Other theories were floated to account for Hilda's behavior, but no one ever dared to ask her why she did what she did. She apparently had no idea how bizarre her co-workers found her no-wine-with-dinner party, nor how her standing took a hit by this decision, nor how long afterward her staff was still referencing the behavior as a benchmark against which to compare other behaviors. It is accurate to say that none of Hilda's direct reports ever felt quite the same way about her after the no-more-wine slight.

INSIGHT

A wine blooper tends to leave an indelible stain in the memories of those who experience or witness one.

The wine-challenged, those who think there's nothing really very complicated about ordering, serving, sharing and drinking wine, are the ones who can get a spot on their reputation that stays there forever.

Take advantage of social events to sample wine. Family gatherings, cocktail parties, events at your clubs or groups to which you belong—celebrations of all types—often include a wine option. Look upon these get-togethers as opportunities to learn more about wine. If nobody in your circle ever drinks wine, you may have to take the initiative and start bringing wine. A paucity of wine drinkers in your circle is also a good excuse to make some new friends, a percentage of whom may be in business and provide an opportunity for meeting even more people. Success in business is aided by expanding your network.

"More wine!"

While the party-animal spirits of Dick, the CEO of the acquiring company in my sixth example, represent the behavioral opposite of Hilda, the negative outcome was just as bad—perhaps worse.

Here the wine-savvy middle managers of two companies, who could not help but draw on their experience, created an object lesson as to why business executives need to know how to pair wine and food. The CEO became the butt of jokes for years afterwards, as meetings of his merged management teams gave rise to wine-food-pairing jokes. Fortunately for Dick, this is still a little-known category of humor. ("Would you like some Ripple with that Grand Marnier Soufflé?" is a recent quip.) The jokes inspired a collection of wisecracks about Dick's real but exaggerated deficiencies in the areas of entertaining, team building, wine-food pairing, wine mentoring and so on. Dick has no idea he is regularly disrespected behind his back because of the way he handled wine that night and on other occasions.

One thing is clear from these stories. Wine ignorance and insensitivity about the finer points of entertaining can create problems for business leaders. Ironically, their fall from grace is a result of good intentions to recognize, to reward, to celebrate. But their good intentions go awry due to the poor quality of their wine skills.

Bear in mind that the top is where—and life's big moments are when—wine should flow most naturally: at hirings, promotions and retirements; at the closing of sales, projects, mergers and acquisitions; at the receiving of awards, grants and patents; at the launching of new products, ventures and IPOs; at the signing of legislation, trade agreements and treaties; at ground-breakings, weddings, births and so on. You name it, wine celebrates the moment.

If you are where the action is, especially if you initiate the action, it is prudent to have wine knowledge to draw on. A lack of experience with wine and wine-related etiquette caused these three senior executives to bewilder and disappoint their guests, undercut the esteem in which they deserved to be held, and damage the uncomplicated loyalty people like to feel toward the company that employs them. Typically, employees do feel unqualified goodwill when they are treated with skill and when recognition of their efforts and accomplishments is handled with class and style.

It is the workaday ordinariness of these six examples that businesspeople should find most unsettling. People with little wine knowledge easily underestimate how damaging the absence of wine skill can be. The *veritas* ancient Romans found *in vino* is more than the true thoughts someone might let slip while in his or her cups. The *veritas* also refers to the truth you can learn about yourself, about others, and about the ways in which wine can help good things happen in a memorable way.

A wine blooper narrated in one of Dorothy J. Gaiter and John Brecher's wine columns in *The Wall Street Journal* leads these wine writers to the observation: "If war is the continuation of politics by another means, wine at business meals is a skirmish...played out on a linen table cloth. Your handling of wine, whether ordering it or just drinking it, matters more than you think to your colleagues..."[6]

We'll return to this thought later in the book.

INSIGHT

The higher your rank, the greater the fall your reputation can take after a public wine blooper.

The business takeaway from Dick's story is that ignorance is not bliss. It can create a reality hidden from you that is detrimental to you personally and perhaps to the reputation of your company. Worst of all, once a wine blooper occurs, it etches a memory in the minds of others that resists erosion. If you know nothing about wine, you might want to make it a policy to delegate wine-related chores to someone with proven wine skills.

There are at least 101 ways to learn about wine. I know because I posted a list of 101 ways on my website *www.wineforbusinesspeople.com* Different folks prefer to gather information in different ways, so visit the site, pick 3 or 4 ways congenial to your personal learning style and start your journey.

CHAPTER IV

Wine Resistance v. Enlightened Self-Development

For those of you responsible for making good things happen in your organization and who want to increase your abilities and effectiveness, but know you are not well informed about wine, the various stories I have told up to this point may motivate you to begin the learning process. That is one of my main goals. If I have achieved it, skip to the next chapter for even more reinforcement.

For others, those of you I have yet to persuade that knowing about wine is a good career move, stay with me a while longer.

In my experience, wine and business often overlap. When they do, the overlapping areas can become, as cited in the previous chapter, "a battlefield on a linen tablecloth." *The Wall Street Journal* writers may overstate the battlefield metaphor, but it has some value. If you are out to dinner with your boss and a peer, how can you be sure well-roundedness vis-à-vis wine is not an item on the boss's checklist, against which to compare you and your peer? He or she may be evaluating you as a candidate for promotion or for more responsibility, such as winning new business, new donors, or new allies in a range of endeavors. Perhaps these responsibilities include entertaining with wine. If you find yourself in a situation like this, wine knowledge will help you avoid tripping a "wine mine" on that battlefield, as one young executive did when she ordered a glass of "rose wine."

Because mine fields exist, and because businesspeople with no background in wine can suddenly find themselves on one, I recommend the protective armament of knowledge. For people in the people end of business, there is simply no good reason not to learn about wine. This is particularly true for those who want to rise in the business world. It is a fact of life that, as you work your way up, you will increasingly encounter people who have made wine a part of their lives. Why this is so is a fascinating subject worthy of exploration. However, that is not an objective of this book. I want only to make the point that knowing how to fully interact with people in the upper strata of business, which means not just on a purely business level, frequently involves knowing how to do a proper job of entertaining others.

I personally extol the value of making wine an ally when entertaining in business. As a consequence of my enthusiasm for wine, I run into differing viewpoints more often than most people. Some of the reasons men and women have given me to justify NOT learning about wine are:

1. "I am successful without wine or business entertaining."

2. "I don't like wine; it just doesn't taste good to me."

3. "Wine drinkers are pretentious; not my kind of people."

4. "I'm too busy. I don't have the time to get into wine."

5. "Worthy causes are more important than wine. I'd rather spend time on that."

6. "Wine is too expensive; I can do the job cheaper with other drinks."

Let's tackle these objections one at a time.

"I am successful without wine."

You can be successful without knowing anything about wine. Some people are. That is not my message. My message is that if you have to sell yourself, your products or services; lead, influence, motivate, hire or develop talent, there are times when wine can help you perform those tasks better. Sometimes much better. That is my point. Why limit yourself?

"Wine doesn't taste good."

It does to countless millions around the world, me included.

Nonetheless, a number of people have told me the taste of wine is unappealing to them. While I personally find this incomprehensible, I don't want to put myself in the position of telling others what tastes good to them. I'd rather side-step that trap in this book. My thesis is only that you will be more successful and certainly more enjoyable to do business with for the wine drinkers among your associates if you integrate wine into your business life. Your efforts to do your job well can be enhanced if you learn how to order and share wine, because that's what some of the people you deal with would like you to do. If you persist in not caring for the taste of wine, let that remain your secret. Just take a token mini-pour in your glass and pretend to take a sip now and then. In my experience, your guests will know how to put your share of the wine to good use and may start to consider you a perfect companion.

"Wine drinkers are pretentious."

Pretentiousness is not in short supply. The world of wine lovers is no exception. Wine snobs are not much different from self-important people who know the batting statistics of every major leaguer who ever played. You don't blame baseball for baseball bores and you shouldn't avoid wine because of wine snobs. They exist and they are easy enough to deal with.

Focus on the fact that it is some people who are pretentious, not wine itself. If, when you ask someone what kind of wine he would like, and he says in a superior tone "ABC" (Anything But Chardonnay), you know you are in for a bumpy ride. The same goes for someone who says: "I only drink French reds" or "No Merlots, please." These people may know even less than you do about wine. They may be trying to mask that they are novices. Or they have heard what the *avant-garde* are saying and want to be included in their number. But even if they know a lot more about wine than you, these are still dumb things to say. The smart thing to say is, "I like Sauvignon Blanc" (no need to malign another grape, just tell us what grape you do like) or (better) "What are our choices?" If you are being entertained in someone's home, the selection may not be wide and you don't want to make your host feel bad for not having your favorite wine on hand.

If Chardonnays had not become so overwhelmingly popular due to their crowd-pleasing drinkability, inspiring some dubious strategies to maximize the market, they wouldn't have inspired such a heavy-duty backlash. French red wines can be delightful, but so can non-French non-red wines. And after the movie *Sideways* gained a critical mass of viewers, hordes of imbibers, overlooking the fact that the Paul Giamatti character was a barely sympathetic loser who was still stealing money from his mother's purse at age 40, kicked off a baseless, lemming-like stampede away from Merlots. People who know wine do not get swept up in fads. They know what they like and confidently stick to their personal taste preferences.

I know about wine snobs primarily from hearsay. Personally, I have had luck with the wine lovers I have met. Almost all of them have had an infectious enthusiasm for wine. They are happy to talk about their experiences with wine, food pairing and their visits to vineyards. In short, they are fun to be with. They are the reason I believe the chapter on wine constitutes some of the more pleasant pages in the book of our civilization.

So, if you have the bad luck to meet a wine snob, first see if you can learn anything useful, and then excuse yourself. Acquiring wine knowledge is simply too smart a move. Don't shortchange wine's potential to assist you because of worries that someone may know more than you and act superior because of it.

"I'm too busy."

I once saw a sign in front of a church that read: "If you're too busy to go to church, you're too busy."

Well said, Reverend!

Concede the points that, one, knowing about wine can be beneficial and, two, that there is much to learn. Acknowledge these two points and—if you are a businessperson—you are likely to recognize the need to carve out time for a bit of learning.

If you truly believe you have no time, one evening curled up with a time-management book can demonstrate the error of that perception. After a trip to the library and a few hours of reading, you will be rewarded with a bushel of practical tips for freeing up time you can put to use learning about wine. And time also for the half dozen other important things in your life you may have been neglecting—such as using wine to help win friends, influence people, and get your career on a faster or better track.

"Worthy causes are more important than wine."

If you donate time and money to worthy charities you have a solid reason to feel good about yourself. If there is little time and discretionary income left after your charitable giving, don't despair. Just keep an eye out for opportunities to experience wine that other people have purchased. Or sample wine in business circumstances where you can legitimately write the entertaining off on your expense account. Also, learn as much as you can in conversations with all the wine drinkers you encounter.

I would emphasize that a percentage of your wealthier and charitably inclined neighbors are likely to be wine drinkers. Like private jets, yachts and fine-art collections, wine cellars are among the trappings the well-to-do acquire to self-actualize. Fluency with wine talk, therefore, provides a conversational entrée when among this cohort. If you speak wine well, you may also find you can be highly effective at steering donations to your favorite charity while in the midst of conversations about where to find the best unoaked California Chardonnays. My wife is a master at this.

"Wine is too expensive."

Compared to what?

Yes, a good bottle of wine is more costly than premium beer or a mixed drink made with top-shelf liquor. Nevertheless, if you are intent on capturing new or expanding existing business, your cause may best be served by entertaining in a fine restaurant with a deep wine cellar. This is a setting where you can effectively demonstrate what a well-rounded person you are, where you can differentiate your enterprise's style from that of other organizations, and where you can make real progress creating a preference on the part of your guest for working with you. Sharing wine over the

> **Wine Fact**
> *The area of the U.S. with the high-est per capita wine consumption is Washington, D.C.; a sobering statistic that may support my case more than I would prefer.* [7]

course of a superior meal has proven to be a productive way to conduct business for me, as well as for many of my clients and associates. We view the cost of this approach more as a strategic investment than an ordinary expense. And wine is the libation of choice in these circumstances because it goes so well with food.

Alternatively, you could invest your sales and marketing dollars in PR, advertising, direct mail, social media, cause-related marketing or other techniques for reaching out to people and winning their hearts and minds. There are many ways to promote your company, though how productive these substantial expenditures are is often hard to pin down. However, a bottle of wine invested in the right person is orders-of-magnitude less expensive than these alternative activities, while only being marginally more expensive than beer and liquor. Moreover, if you are trying to do business with someone who likes wine—or is open to learning about wine—and who is also a good prospect, entertaining with wine has a high likelihood of helping you connect successfully. Think of wine expenditures as one of the smarter components of your GS&A budget and use these outlays as the stepping stones to establishing valuable relationships.

*　　*　　*

If any of these objections were in your mind at the start of this chapter I hope I have overcome them. Wine works. Using wine over the years has kept my business humming along and made the journey much more fun than it would otherwise have been—for me, for my clients, and for my associates.

Now that I have convinced most of my readers that using wine in business is a capital idea, you might want to consider how you will shape the journey that takes you to wine knowledge. For some, the educational process is slow, easy and painless; for others, fast and hard.

Here are stories of two people who experienced very different wine-initiation journeys.

The Gourmet Group

"In the beginning, I had no use for wine. It was never part of my personal history. One day my wife and two neighbors decided life would be incomplete if they didn't form a gourmet group. Their plan was to stop dreaming about the fancy meals they wanted to serve their families and actually learn how to cook them. They would divide up the dishes, match them with wine and open their houses once a month on a rotating basis for a feast. The husbands would be their guinea pigs.

"When my wife warned me one summer that it was our turn to host the dinner, I suggested we have some gin, vodka and tonic on hand so the guys wouldn't have to drink any of those sissy white wines with the appetizer course. She smiled sweetly and explained that our choices for the appetizer course that evening would be white wine A or white wine B.

"Over the months, the wives really did teach themselves how to cook impressive meals. They also figured out how to get us to look forward to drinking wine and how to talk about wine and food. As the meals got better, my suggestions for wine substitutes ceased. But this was a social thing. It didn't have anything to do with business.

"Later, after years of training by the gourmet group, there was a wrangle at a business dinner over how to maximize our wine dollar when some people wanted fish, some meat, and some poultry. I asked the host for the wine list, and, drawing on my years of experience with the gourmet group, came up with a solution in a few minutes that satisfied everyone.

"One of my companions said, 'I had no idea you knew so much about wine.' I murmured humbly, 'Well, I guess it had to come out some time.' From that point on, I was the company wine expert."

Director of Quality
Foundry
Milwaukee, WI

That's one way people get into wine. Here's another:

The Roast

"I work in a department of a big financial services company where, on any given day, the guy who shows the roughest sense of humor scores the most points. I had just received a promotion and the six other guys in my department took me out for dinner afterwards to celebrate. That night I was pretty full of myself and saying a lot of outrageous things for the fun of it. I can't remember now what I actually said halfway through the dinner, but one of the guys countered with, 'Well, what can you expect from the only guy at the table drinking beer!'

"I looked around the table. Sure enough. The other six were all drinking wine. I looked up and into their eyes. Given our work culture, if I may use that term, I suddenly felt like a bleeding baitfish tossed into a pool of starving sharks. A line of attack opened in six brains with me in the middle as the target. I knew I was in for it.

"One guy swirled the wine in his glass and gave me the evil eye. 'He didn't get the memo.' His phrasing suggested a grisly fatality that might have been avoided. A friend rose in false defense. 'No, all his personal holdings are beer companies. He's just doing his part to make them successful.' 'And besides that, he's loyal,' said another, 'he only accepts clients with more than $500,000 to invest who drink beer exclusively.' For some reason, the group found this particularly funny. After the laughter died down, it went right back up when another colleague referenced my fraternity and said 'When they graduate, all those guys get the house-beer logo tattooed in their armpits and take an oath never to drink anything else.'

"This gross falsehood prompted another associate to observe, 'I don't see Roger getting tattoos in any sensitive places—he's too afraid of pain. I think it's a case of arrested development.'

"'Whoa! Hold on there,' my best friend in the department said, pretending to leap to my defense when someone had gone too far. He didn't fool me for a second. There is no such thing as 'too far' when this crowd gets going.

"'You remember after his last party,' here my best friend was overcome by laughter. I couldn't remember anything funny about my last party. As I watched everybody laughing it occurred to me it wasn't a memory of something that happened before that was funny. They were already laughing in anticipation of the zinger to come.

"'He showed then he's not arrested! He developed from DOMESTIC BEER IN CANS,' he choked on laughter briefly, and then shouted so the whole restaurant could hear, 'to IMPORTED BEER IN BOTTLES!'

"Up until this moment, my party had been a little raucous, but nothing so out of bounds that the waitstaff would become alarmed. But now everybody at the table was howling.

"I sensed, incorrectly, that the worst was over and wanted to say something to reclaim my dignity. 'Ha, ha, very funny,' is what came out. I admit this wasn't original. Under pressure, I'll even admit that it was totally witless. Actually, it was worse. My feeble sarcasm was like throwing gasoline on a fire. My words turned out to be as ill-advised as my drink order. The laughter simply exploded out of control.

"Our waiter came over shouting, 'Gentlemen! Gentlemen! Gentlemen!' He was trying to bring the riot under control. 'Can I get anyone anything?'

"That's when the guy who started it all with the comment about me not getting the memo achieved departmental immortality by saying, 'Yeah! Bring us a wine glass with training wheels!'

"I sat there, ears burning. Promoted up and roasted way back down, all in one day. I looked at my co-workers. Heads thrown back, each had a waterfall of tears streaming down his face. I could see the fillings in everyone's teeth. The laughter was so irresistible most of the people at nearby tables couldn't help joining in. By then, some survival mechanism in my subconscious must have kicked in, because I was laughing louder than anyone.

"You asked me how I got into wine. This is how I got into wine."

Account Manager
Financial Services
Chicago, IL

INSIGHT

I think these last two examples show that there are benefits and risks related to wine in business.

In light of these stories, I will float the idea that you should not consider yourself a well-rounded businessperson if you lack basic wine skills. I offer one more observation, as a last point in this part of my case: In a fundamental sense, this argument is not about you, but about the people who can help you succeed and who also like wine. Developing the skill to use wine with this group is an enlightened thing to do. Ultimately, it's all about how they, not you, feel about wine. It's about how they fit wine into their business world and, on the basis of that, how you might come to fit into their world.

In the next chapter, let's look at the power of wine to help make good things happen.

The Internet is an inexhaustible source of information about wine. Type "wine" in the address bar of your browser and you may get 491,000,000 results in 0.08 seconds, as I just did.[8]

CHAPTER V

Wine Success Stories

My associates who are fans of using wine when entertaining for business are happy to talk to me about it—but off the record.

One reason is their desire not to create the impression that they have over-engineered their customers' wine experiences. Wine works best when it simply flows into the scene in a natural and unforced way. Many of my friends work hard at adding to their wine knowledge and honing their skill at entertaining with wine. But they don't want to be perceived as working hard at wine. Wine is supposed to be one of life's rewarding pleasures, not something one "works at."

A second reason is they consider business entertaining with wine a powerful but easily imitated trade secret—they don't want their competition to learn any more than they already know about their winning ways. So they don't call attention to this practice.

A third reason is that wine is an alcoholic beverage. Alcohol should be treated with respect and discretion in business. It should support an executive's entertainment style, not be the main event or call too much attention to itself.

A fourth reason is that talking enthusiastically about wine in business might sound to your boss like you are having too much fun when you ought to be "working." Not all managers are enlightened on this subject.

So, here, speaking off the record, is what a few of my clients and associates have to say about entertaining with wine.

"Enriching business get-togethers."

"When Bill told me about his idea for a book about wine in business, I was concerned his voice would be lost in a chorus of others. We are both dedicated wine users in our business lives and have been sharing stories with each other for years. I could not believe that there was not already a rich trove of information, books and articles on this topic. To me it is obviously a great subject.

"After our meeting, I went online. I Googled 'wine in business.' I came up with very little information of the type Bill and I discussed, although if I ever want to buy some used barrels or bulk grape juice, I now know where to go. Later, on a trip to my local book store, I found many wine books and many business books, but no 'wine-in-business' books.

"Then I told Bill I thought he may be onto something. He asked me to tell him what I thought about wine in business. Here it is, as short and sweet as I can make it:

"In the course of doing business, I discovered that a whole lot of people at the top rungs enjoyed wine and knew a great deal about it. I wanted to live my business life at the top rung and systematically educated myself about wine to help get me there. My reliance on wine when entertaining customers helped me and my team to sell literally billions of dollars of my company's products during the extended period I was in charge of sales. Doing business at the top typically involves relating to sophisticated people whose day jobs include the purchase of the things I sell. Meetings with these people provided a permanent stream of opportunities for business meals. Wine is a natural element for enriching business get-togethers. So much so that it became a constant feature of the approach I developed for doing business."

President/CEO
Aerospace Manufacturing
Portland, OR

"The quality experience our customers have."

"At my company, our people have a tradition of uncorking wine when entertaining customers, particularly with our company's Asian customers, many of whom cultivate an appreciation of the finer things in life and want to experience them when traveling on business to our facilities in the U.S. and Europe. When these customers pay us a visit, we make sure we have a number of after-hours and weekend activities to provide a change of scene. Our goal is to create opportunities to get to know each other—or get to know each other better—because most of these customers we have worked with for years.

"How do I know integrating wine into our business entertainment has been successful? I personally know this because customers, after a few glasses of wine—and in contrast to all the clichés about Oriental indirectness and subtlety—have looked me in the eye and told me straight-out what a pleasure it is to visit us on business. Imagine how good I felt whenever I heard this and I have heard it a number of times in almost these exact words.

"To make my dealings with customers memorable, I have always paid special attention to food and wine. I study the wines I plan to recommend for specific customers at specific restaurants. That way, I have an assortment of interesting things to talk about. For me, using wine in business meets two objectives. First, it gives you a break from business. It offers a way to relax and spend time with people who matter in your life. I can't overemphasize how important this point is for success with people. Second, while it is not something we mention but are nonetheless highly conscious of, entertaining with style is a part of the quality of the experience our customers have working with us. We knock ourselves out to make sure that quality experience happens."

VP International Sales
Defense Industry Supplier
New York, NY

"Forging a spirited, hard-working team."

"I am on the corporate staff of my company and although I don't have sales or investor-relations responsibilities, I still find all sorts of ways to use my love of wine in my job.

"My most recent wine adventure was during my participation on a special project on the West Coast. It involved one of our departments that had just been assigned a new manager. In addition to a number of routine tasks, I was also along to facilitate the interaction among five, long-term department members, all of whom I knew well, and their new boss.

"Let me cut to the chase: the team did a great job on a four-day assignment and as we all gathered to let off steam at the end of the project, I indulged my passion for wine by persuading the new department head the team deserved a really great bottle of wine—one of California's finest costing a couple of hundred bucks a bottle.

"The team watched as the boss gave my recommendation only a moment's silent debate (expense-account austerity is the watchword these days) before shouting: 'You're darn right the team deserves something special!'

"We doled out the wine in equal measures and sat back to enjoy it. It was sublime. I'd had the wine before so planned to nurse my pour as long as possible. But the others, possibly shocked by how good it was, couldn't resist drinking it quickly.

"Then one of the team members said rather sheepishly: 'Boss, that bottle didn't go very far with so many of us. Do you think we could possibly order another?' There was sort of a pleading note in his voice. Pleasure that intense should not be that fleeting.

"The department head entered a short period of thoughtfulness. It's one thing to put through an expense account group meal with a $200 bottle of wine in it. It's another thing to try to push through two bottles for $400 not counting tip and taxes. However, the moment was unique. The new boss and his team were on a roll. They had coalesced professionally before my eyes over a short, four-day period. What's the real cost of wine measured against forging a spirited, hard-working team, I wondered? At that moment, it seemed to me as if the deci-sion might set the tone for the team for the entire future it would have together.

"After very little internal debate, he softly said: 'Let's do it.' The die was cast. Another bottle was ordered. While I was hypothesizing how he might finesse the wine on his expense account, the waiter came back and said, 'Sorry, sir. That was the last bottle.'

"We all groaned, but the new man had already earned the goodwill of his team. Everybody now felt as if he or she was a member of a tightly knit group. Together, we shared a fond memory of the first bottle and the loss of the second.

"Wine will do this sort of thing. Other kinds of drinks can't."

Manager, Information Services
Aerospace Systems Manufacturer
Boston, MA

"Great wine paired with great food will win over almost everyone."

"The most remarkable story I have about the seductive power of wine came early in my career. As an account executive at a large advertising and public-relations agency, I entertained clients regularly and typically drank wine at dinner. One of my clients, the director of communications for one of our business-to-business accounts, happened to be a World War II veteran, dedicated golfer and an adamant non-wine drinker. His drink of choice was a martini and he would drink two or three of them during the course of a meal. Despite our differing preferences for drinks, he took me under his wing and treated me like a son because I was a Vietnam veteran and equally addicted golfer and we had those bonds between us. But over all the time we worked together I was never able to interest him in sharing a bottle of wine.

"On the eve of his retirement, I invited him and his wife out to dinner. His wife picked the restaurant, nationally famous and a local legend, and I prepared myself for a pleasant evening. I remember having a quick conversation with the sommelier about the best wine in his cellar to go with the rack of lamb I planned to order. I was careful not to drag out this part of the evening with two martini drinkers as guests.

"The sommelier suggested a Bordeaux, and said he had some excellent vintages in the cellar. I told him this was a special meal and that he should pick what he thought would be the best wine under $100. I turned to my guests who looked askance at my extravagance. 'I'm going to miss you and this is my consolation prize,' I explained.

"When the wine was served I was simply blown away by how fantastic it was. With many years of wine drinking now behind me I can state it was the best wine I ever drank and that I have never found its equal.

"I was so smitten with the wine that I insisted my guests sample a small taste to see what a pleasant experience I was having and they were missing. Besides, I didn't want to drink the whole bottle by myself and never carry uncorked wine out of a restaurant.

> **Wine Fact**
> *The U.S. will purchase more than 300 million cases of wine in 2012.*[9]

"Because I was insistent, they agreed to gag down a few drops to humor me. That's when a strange thing happened. Both my client and his wife commented it was one of the best things they had ever tasted in their whole lives.

"I was unprepared for this complete conversion in one or two sips, but that's what happened. My guests proceeded to finish off the entire bottle with the appetizer course, emptying it just as the entrées were served. Fortunately, I had secured a decent pour when one or the other didn't have his or her hand on the bottle.

"I drank my glass very slowly and pondered the irony of working with someone who for years would not touch wine, then, when I had a Bordeaux fit for a king in front of me, Mr. and Mrs. Martini became total wine converts. Bad timing for me, but a good lesson for me, too: Lead people to wine and make them drink it. A great wine paired with great food will win over almost everyone with functioning taste buds. Once you convert them, you won't have to spend years limiting your experiences because your guests think they don't like wine."

VP Client Services
Advertising and PR Agency
Chicago

"Has wine helped me be successful? Yes."

"I am past traditional retirement age but still active in business. I was born in what was Czechoslovakia, grew up in a second country, and served in the military of a third. Along the way I picked up many languages. When I got into business after University, I used my languages on behalf of American companies. I helped them make deals with European customers, suppliers and partners in many different kinds of ventures.

"My work eventually brought me to the aerospace industry, where everybody speaks English. For example, when Germans in the aerospace industry visit companies in the German-speaking part of Switzerland, everybody speaks English! I became worried I soon would not be able to trade on my language skills in aerospace. That's when I began to appreciate more my skill with wine.

"In truth, most Americans businesspeople don't spend much time thinking about wine. Only a few Americans I have worked with are good at ordering wine for Europeans. They defer to Europeans—and give up a little power when they do so. Among this small number, an even smaller percentage of Americans have taken the trouble to master wine. However, when making deals in complex situations, across cultures and sometimes multiple companies, it became clear to me that my ability to create a relaxing setting was valuable. My clients needed an atmosphere where the human side of deals and the necessary back and forth between participants could take place more easily than they could in a conference room. If I could set up this atmosphere it would be of benefit to them.

"My clients would say: 'Pick a restaurant and take care of all the details so we can concentrate on the important things.' Once, after I had sent back a bottle of wine, one of my clients thanked me for sparing his guest a bad wine. 'We like the way you look out for us,' he said. I saw that wine could be a useful part of my service. I looked out for clients at the crossroads of different business cultures. That was the thing they appreciated.

"If I didn't know my wine, I would not have had the confidence to do the best possible job. During my career, I became good at picking and serving European wines at long lunches and dinners. Now that I am an American citizen, I am learning about American wines.

"So, has wine helped me be successful? Yes. Definitely. What's more, I like my business so much I don't want to stop working. I have gotten good at what I do and one part of what I do best is help my clients entertain successfully."

Principal
International Aerospace Consultancy
Phoenix, AZ

"$300 a bottle? Worth every last nickel."

"Memorable business entertainment has always been a part of our firm's customer-relations strategy. It's a way to show we appreciate the business. Fine wine is always a part of that strategy. It's a given that you are doing great work for your client—without that, business entertainment doesn't mean much with or without wine. While it is hard to prove a one-to-one link between top-notch entertaining and a long-term profitable relationship, it is an assumption we've always worked on and it always seems to work for us.

"As I see it, superb, occasional entertainment—in other words, a wonderful dinner with sophisticated choices of wine—is a matter of 'doing things right.' It reflects the same kind of thinking that means fifth-row center seats at a Broadway show. A wonderful wine at dinner may prompt passing appreciative comments from a non-wine person. However, if the client is a wine connoisseur, it's an entirely different story.

"I well remember when my two partners and I took out a client and her husband for a very expensive (and very good) dinner at a top New York City restaurant. I know a bit about wine, but one of my partners was our resident expert, having taken the wine course offered by the Windows on the World. I asked him to do the wine honors.

"W-e-l-l, the wine was beyond spectacular and we had six bottles for the evening to cover eight people. As you might imagine, the bill for wine and dinner was astronomical. That didn't particularly bother me because my attitude towards client entertainment has always been to do it infrequently, but do it extremely well—something they'd talk about afterwards.

"The next day I asked my wine-maven partner how much the wine cost (I was thinking about laying in a lifetime supply of the wine he had selected). He said, 'You don't want to know.' I replied, 'Oh yes, I DO want to know!' (I had the reputation of being careful about money.)

"His answer was, '$300 a bottle.' My response was, 'Worth every last nickel.'"

Managing Partner
Advertising Agency
New York, NY

One of the things that aided and abetted my interest in wine is my love of maps. One of my favorite wine maps is my well-used copy of Rand McNally's *A Guide to the Wine Country: California*. I have rarely made a trip to northern California without using it to visit wineries in Napa, Sonoma and Mendocino counties. The Santa Barbara County Vintners' Association published a handy wine touring map I picked up in 1998 and still use when I visit southern California.

One thing I find very irksome is to discover that I have been somewhere and driven right by or close to a winery I didn't know existed. To my mind, that's truly a wasted opportunity. Now before any business trip, I check to see if I'll be close to a winery or tasting room—and I do my best to carve out time for a quick visit.

"More energy to vent than a hurricane."

"Some transformations in business are so significant that they cry out for a Champagne ceremony.

"A few years back, working as a consultant in a Canadian manufacturing company, my team ran into a wall of resistance to change. The company still had pockets of the outdated mass-production mindset in place at the very worst time.

"The company was losing business and the needed change was hampered when layoffs wiped out the low-seniority younger workers (those least resistant to change) and kept in place the most senior workers (those most resistant to change).

"Even with a cooperative union, the legacy of old work rules prevented progress. At one machining center, a true disaster materialized. A senior machinist, struggling to adapt unfamiliar lean manufacturing principles, alien work procedures and a new computer-controlled machining program updated to accommodate an improved setup technique, scrapped 11 parts in a row. The company had almost US$100,000 apiece in sunk-cost invested in these expensive aerospace components before they arrived at this work cell—and every last one of them had been rendered unusable.

"This situation was an embarrassment for everybody involved and dozens of us, including shop-floor managers and a bunch of grim-faced interested parties with video cameras from the corporate office, swarmed that work cell. The company representative involved in training the trainers, the person responsible for taking the new ideas throughout the entire factory, was getting quite emotional about all the high-level attention.

"I know Bill asked me to say something about wine, not the history of a Canadian manufacturer, but you really can't appreciate this as a business story without having a sense of the big dollars, regional pride and future stakes involved for this company. There was a whole lot on the line and we all wanted to make the changes work, show progress and hold the gains.

"OK, long story gets short. We did it. And the pent-up emotion after we demonstrated that we could machine the next batch of parts flawlessly was explosive.

So the entire team headed straight for the nearest bar after work. We ordered up a case of good French Champagne (readily at hand; we were in Québec) and had a rip-roaring celebration led by the guy responsible for training the trainers who had more energy to vent than a hurricane.

"To me, the Champagne blowout unofficially certified the group's acceptance of a new way of doing work. This boisterous, paid-for-with-our-own-money celebration stabilized the chaotic feelings within the company. After absorbing the triple shocks of right-sizing, reorganizing and reengineering, everybody now knew the hard part was over. The Champagne ceremony put closure on the change process and drew the whole shop together as a new, improved team."

Turnaround Specialist
Management Consultancy
New Haven, CT

"Vive le vin!"

"My work as a management consultant has brought me to some far-flung places and into contact with different cultures. On the subject of wine in business, one experience stands out. After one of my American clients snapped up a factory in northwestern France as part of a mega-global acquisition, I was parachuted in to figure out why this particular unit was losing money.

"One of the first things that struck me as out of line was that, on the day I and my team were introduced to the employees, they had laid out a magnificent French-style lunch. In the employee cafeteria, all the tables had white tablecloths. Each had a bottle of wine at the center, surrounded by nice wine glasses, china, silverware and cloth napkins. Professional-looking chefs wearing white toques and spotless aprons milled about preparing to serve us. We felt honored.

"The next day the scene was repeated. I felt such hospitality was over the top and asked them not go to the trouble the next day. They looked at me uncomprehendingly. At last one of them explained: '*Mais, monsieur,* this is not for you. We do this every day.'

"My first reaction was that I had discovered why they were not making any money. They were being fed in high style by the company and literally eating and drinking away the profits. I planned to find evidence to support this perception and put a stop to this wasteful practice.

"By way of background, the French workers were not excited about having their factory sold to Americans. Stories of ruthlessly efficient, heartless capitalism American-style are common in Europe. However, the former French owner had started the inevitable and long overdue process of laying off workers and they knew their operation was in trouble. Something had to and would be done. On top of that, they knew that they probably wouldn't like what had to be done.

"This is when things started to get interesting. I quickly discovered that the cost of feeding the employees lunch was chicken feed compared to the cost of running the entire operation with seriously [and boy do I mean seriously!] obsolete production strategies. So rather than start by taking away their rolls and butter, we pointed the cost-cutting knife where we would earn the biggest and fastest return. This turned out to be a brilliant approach, though I had no idea of it at the time.

"What happened over the weeks and months that followed was amazing. I watched a group of people who, when the lunch bell rang, all went to the cafeteria together. There was no hierarchy. Everything was quite egalitarian. The plant manager sat next to the janitor one day. It was one big happy family at lunch time. Everyone was from the same town. All were literally neighbors—and a lot of them were seriously ticked off at the changes being demanded of them. But all of that was put on hold at lunch time. They all shared food and wine with each other and with us, they talked about life at work and life in the village. In a word, it was all very civilized.

"Eventually, things came to a head regarding demanded changes. New ideas hadn't yet had a chance to demonstrate a swing to profitability—how could they, in three or four short weeks. So the workers decided to go on strike.

"The union people at the table all talked about the upcoming strike with us at lunch, all very amicably, and almost apologetically they informed us exactly what to expect. Then, at two o'clock that day, the workers shut off their machines, put on their caps and walked out the door.

"For the next 10 minutes, they stood outside the factory and smoked cigarettes. Then, after 10 minutes, they all returned to their stations and went back to work. It was really quite astonishing. And it was all so civilized. I still don't quite understand how it could have happened the way it did, but happen it did.

"We knew the employees were filled with uncertainty about the future, about the American ideas that were supposed to save them from being shut down, about the stressful changes they would all have to go through if things didn't work. We had a great deal of empathy for them, because we'd been having lunch with them every day for weeks and knew exactly how they felt. Their concerns had become our concerns and we addressed them as sincerely and persuasively as we could.

"That tradition of sitting down every day at the lunch table (we never ate in the executive dining room in another part of the facility), of sharing a glass of wine and a tasty lunch, just civilized the heck out of all of us. Over the short couple of months we were there, the employees came around to a new way of thinking about their work and set themselves on a path to profitability—without sacrificing the lunches they proved they could earn.

"If OSHA had been there to ban the wine, I'm not sure things would have worked out so positively.

"Vive le vin!"

Lean Manufacturing Consultant
International Management Consulting Company
Portland, ME

"Suddenly, we had a problem."

"This is my best wine story: We were at a get-together one of our customers held annually in Denver. My partner and I were looking forward to having a good time meeting a lot of people we mostly just talked to on the phone all year.

"Our firm was the company's designated sole source for food packaging. The managers at all of the company's regional offices were required to work with us. It was a solid business relationship. Everything was copacetic. Or so we thought.

"Out of the blue, one of our sponsors in the head office mentioned that a number of the regional managers were grousing about being 'forced' to work with us. Apparently, many of them wanted to work with local suppliers who called on them regularly soliciting business. Suddenly, we had a problem.

"Our sponsor, my partner and I convened a hasty, stand-up meeting, bounced the problem around for a couple of minutes and sped off in three directions, I to a nearby restaurant we knew was promoting an oyster festival, my partner to the hotel's business center and the sponsor to his hotel room to get us a list of the regional managers' names and addresses.

"Thanks to cell phones and stick drives, within a half hour, the first annual Oyster and Chardonnay Dinner was organized, invitations printed and envelopes addressed. My partner and I carried the invitations back to the conference and distributed them to the invitees within an hour.

"The restaurant we picked had a wide selection of Chardonnays, a wine I like, and we made sure wine from many different vineyards would be available. The idea was to get everybody talking about which Chardonnay goes best with oysters Rockefeller, which one with oysters casino, raw oysters, fried oysters and so on.

"People who had never before tasted an oyster and people who rarely ordered wine were all drawn in to the spirit of the evening. Before we knew it, everybody was talking, sharing opinions, eating, drinking and having a good time. Through the course of the dinner, we made sure everybody got to know us better. It was all social—no business.

"The event was such a success we repeated it year after year at the customer's annual meeting. Word spread about our invitation-only Oyster and Chardonnay Dinner and a lot of people started dropping hints well before the meeting that they would love to be invited. The mountain of empty half-shells increased every year and the unrest among the regional managers about the supplier mandate was washed away by a tide of Chardonnay.

"When a business arrangement looks like it has wheels coming off, food, wine and fun are a great way to tighten things back up quickly."

Partner
Food Packaging Company
Shawnee Mission, KS

"You already know how to pick good wines."

"Over the course of my years in sales and marketing, I developed an extensive history of entertaining clients. During the early part of my career, it was clear beer or hard liquor were the drinks of choice for these kinds of occasions.

"But as I grew in my job, and as my experiences and responsibilities broadened to include more travel and the opportunity to meet an international community of professionals, I was increasingly exposed to the role of wine in business. However, it wasn't until I was assigned to Paris as director of international sales, and became a full-fledged expatriate, that I learned how central wine can be to doing business with the right attention to style. To my surprise, I found that a 'wine-in-business' culture manifested itself at all levels in Europe, including non-management staff. I was amazed to learn how much wine know-how there was out there and the extent to which it had established itself as a natural and common element of everyday life.

"After just a few days in my new position, I became aware that my minimal knowledge and previous experience with wine were wholly inadequate to meet the challenges I would face in this environment. I was a little intimidated, for sure, but determined to rise to the challenge. The path forward was suggested by my wife, who always seems to offer me the 'why didn't I think of that' type of ideas I need. At her prompting, I enrolled in an evening wine-tasting course designed for 'ex-pats' who were trying to assimilate into this way of life.

"During the first week of the course, I made a major adjustment to my natural instincts by learning how to spit out great-tasting wine, so I could standby in sober, unimpaired readiness to sample my next mouthful. By the second week, I knew how to appreciate the nuances of color, appearance and aroma. And by the third week, my nose could pick out the smells of flowers, fruit and 'barnyard.' Beyond that, I learned how to think about the ways individual wines would mate up with certain foods. Our instructor taught us how to find good-vintage years and how to avoid the bad ones. Not trusting our memories, he gave us a reference table to carry around for future use. At the conclusion of the course, I was certainly no wine expert, but I did feel much more confident that I'd be able to select the right wine when I had to.

"It didn't take long for me to reap the benefits of my fast-track wine education. The first chance to pass/fail presented itself in the form of a dinner engagement with one of our company's most promising European prospects. This senior executive was responsible for the total procurement activity of a very large global manufacturing company. Obviously, establishing a good relationship with this person would be critical to our future success in that industry.

"As the junior executive at this meeting, my boss, who flew in from the U.S. for the meeting and the after-hours get-together, delegated the task of hosting the dinner to me, instructing me to find a suitable restaurant in Paris. At the start of the dinner, he suggested I select the wines for the evening. This was truly a test! Luckily for me, there were five of us at the dinner that evening. By just the number of guests alone, I knew I had the basis for ordering more than one bottle. The number made it easy for me to order both a white and a red, without asking what kind of food my guests were planning to eat.

"The wine list was extensive, offering a varied array of excellent choices. With a sense of relief, I recognized some of the very same wines I had learned about in my tasting course. I chose a white Bordeaux and a red Burgundy in the median price range. I thought that would give my guests the widest number of choices when selecting the dish they would order for dinner.

"When the wine arrived, I tested the white and asked my boss to approve the red. I didn't know if this was the right thing to do, but he responded enthusiastically and endorsed the wine I chose. The dinner turned out to be successful at laying the foundation of a relationship that continues to this day. That night we drank two bottles of each of the wines I had selected, and everyone complimented me on the choices I made. But the greatest satisfaction came when our special guest bid me, *'Bonsoir.'* He added: 'I can see you are fitting well into your new assignment here in France. You already know how to pick good wines.'"

Director International Sales
Aerospace Component Manufacturer
Darien, CT

INSIGHT

Businesspeople really do want to be successful.

These 10 stories support my thesis. I know my associates seek success, because I know each personally and have observed their winning ways for years.

Wine knowledge definitely helps businesspeople be successful.

These stories show that wine has played a positive role in the careers of many of my associates. Wine has also proved helpful at smoothing out rough spots in business. Wine knowledge is practical. Businesspeople who acquire it possess a tool with great potential. Without doubt, businesspeople benefit from using their wine knowledge.

To my thinking, these 10 examples clinch my argument that wine knowledge is valuable in business. Moreover, I believe there are hundreds, maybe thousands, of wine-in-business stories out there that further amplify my claims.

This belief underpins Bill's Second Law of Wine in Business, which is that wine has the power to make things happen.

On the strong belief that wine-in-business anecdotes abound, I invite you to share your wine epiphanies, wine bloopers and wine-success stories. Join the discussion on my blog: **www.wineforbusinesspeople.com**

CHAPTER VI

Decision Time

It is time now for you to judge whether I have made the case for wine.

I have argued that knowing about wine gives you a useful business skill.

I have told stories about young executives with services, products or ideas to sell who discovered that wine can rise up as a challenge during the sales process and who made the commitment to be better prepared for their next wine encounter.

I have told stories about senior executives who lacked the know-how to make a business event involving wine an experience memorable for the right reasons. Unfortunately, like Disney's sorcerer's apprentice, these otherwise capable managers were not in true control of the situations they created. They seemed unaware that their good intentions fell flat. Sadly, these executives had no idea of the extent to which perceptions of each of them as a business leader were damaged by their handling of wine.

Last, I have reported on associates who know wine and use it routinely in business. They know wine has helped them do their job effectively. These wine-savvy executives have succeeded because, at a minimum, in any wine situation they acquit themselves well, or, at the maximum, because they consciously integrate wine into their business lives, create opportunities to use wine, and apply their skills and entertainment strategies to accomplish a multitude of objectives.

Beyond this, I have offered a few tips to start building your wine knowledge.

Wine Fact
The U.S. now spends more than $30 billion per year on wine. [10]

I hope my stories have resolved any lingering doubts you may have had about the value of wine in business. Beyond that, I hope you will give wine a chance to complement your future meals, so you can discover what tastes best to you when you bring food and wine together. I also hope you look forward to the pleasant outcomes that can result from sharing wine, forging deeper connections and cementing long-term, profitable relationships in business.

If you make wine one of your skills, I trust that a bit of magic will happen along the way. First, that you will come to discover that wine makes food taste better and vice versa. This is reason enough to begin your journey. Second, that this discovery will give you all the motivation you need to make a life-long commitment to learning about wine. And third, that you will enjoy the rewards of learning about wine in many areas of your life.

There may still be a few who say wine is an optional item on the list of critical business skills. But why deny yourself the confidence and versatility that is the natural accompaniment of knowing about wine?

Consider the Gaiter-Brecher comment made in their article about the risk to businesspeople who do not do wine well:

"Unfortunately, sometimes people see your comfort or experience with wine not as a comment on your knowledge, but on your character." [11]

That's what they say.

Ouch!

Can someone's character be judged by his or her level of wine knowledge? In a sense, it can. Gaiter and Brecher are making a crucial point. Fair or not, people make judgments about you all the time. When a wine-knowledgeable senior person observes a subordinate who demonstrates that he or she knows little or nothing about wine, that shortcoming is noted.

As one CEO who watches closely the development of his people said, "Wine is an indicator. It's one of the ways people who know about it communicate they are prepared for predictable contingencies. When I see it, it gives me confidence in them. I can imagine them in situations where wine skill is called for and visualize them handling themselves in a satisfactory manner. That's reassuring. Conversely, when that skill is lacking, I notice that too, and have concerns about the impression that person will create when representing our firm with customers across the whole range of business situations."

Ask yourself whether you have a gap where others have a space filled with personal experiences and a stock of knowledge. If such a gap exists, it is likely to reveal itself sooner or later, particularly if you are pursuing professional growth, seeking advancement in your organization, and striving to establish a personal history for making positive things happen.

When a gap reveals itself, it is noted by others around you—clients, customers, associates, bosses, peers, subordinates—people who themselves may already have closed that gap. In that moment, another perception about the kind of person you are will be etched into their minds. Repeated evidence of this gap results in perceptions that can prove impossible to erase and difficult to change.

I rest my case.

April 10, 2012
Santiago, Mexico

Notes

1. *www.decanter.com* March 16, 2011.

2. *www.wineinstitute.org*
   Search "Quick Links" on the homepage.

3. *The Economist,* "Octobergloom," p. 76, October 9, 2010.

4. *www.depts.ttu.edu*
   Use the search option to find: US wine consumption trends

5. Barbara Insel, *Understanding Wine Demographics in a Down Market,*
   www.winebusiness.com/wbm/?go=getArticleSignIn&dataId=62896

6. Dorothy J. Gaiter and John Brecher, "'Boss, May I Suggest the Lancers?'
   and Other Wine Bloopers in Business Settings", *The Wall Street Journal,*
   May 5, 2000.

7. *www.drvino.com/2007/09/27/washington-dc-is-the-thirstiest-non-state-in-america*

8. Google search conducted on December 8, 2011, 4:30pm ET.

9. The US will purchase 300 million cases of wine in 2012.
   Source: *www.decanter.com* December 2011.

10. U.S. spent $30 billion on wine in 2010. *www.wineinstitute.org/resources/pressroom/03152011*

11. Gaiter, Brecher, "Boss, May I Suggest the Lancers?"

Note on the notes

Wine statistics change by the hour and are updated slowly. Follow the published statistics in the websites above to give yourself a general understanding of which countries are major players and what various rankings and trends are in wine production and consumption.

Put the Power of Wine to Work When Entertaining Clients and Customers

Bring one of Bill's seminars to your location.

Learn the many ways organizations benefit from insuring their rainmakers are comfortable and confident using wine in business.

Gain insight through case-study examples into a range of client-relations successes that have accrued to firms that have mastered the art of entertaining with wine.

Discover the competitive advantages that derive from entertaining with wine in business—from inspiring intense client loyalty to effectively locking out competitors.

Guide life-long learning of productive business-development and client-relations skills based on wine know-how and well-managed entertaining techniques.

See how a company's identity and reputation are enhanced when associates are skilled with wine and know how to use it with prospects, clients or customers.

Author Bill Libby's seminars and integrated wine-training/rainmaking programs are described at *www.wineforbusinesspeople.com*

Contact Bill at *blibby@libbycom.com* or **203-820-6655**.

www.ingramcontent.com/pod-product-compliance
Lightning Source LLC
Chambersburg PA
CBHW041102180526
45172CB00001B/73